# SHAPES

# IN NATURE
## BY JUDY FELDMAN

CHILDRENS PRESS ®

CHICAGO

The cover and title page image is a land snail.
© Bill Christensen/Root Resources

Series cover and interior design by Sara Shelton

Library of Congress Cataloging-in-Publication Data

Feldman, Judy.
  Shapes in nature/by Judy Feldman.
     p.     cm.—(Wordless concept books)
  Summary: Explores the world of shapes through photographs of nature.
  ISBN 0-516-05102-4
  1. Geometry—Juvenile literature.   2. Nature—Pictorial works—
Juvenile literature. [1. Nature—Pictorial works.   2. Shape.]
I. Title.  II. Series.
QA445.5.F44   1991
516'.15—dc20                                               90-23091
                                                               CIP
                                                               AC

A mountain and its reflection, Jasper National Park, Alberta, Canada
© Pam Hickman/Valan

Four robin's eggs in a nest
© Jerry Hennen

Candy cane seastar on coral in the Red Sea
© Jeff Rotman

A sponge grows among coral
© Jeff Rotman

A school of cow rays near the Galápagos Islands
© Jeff Rotman

The beautiful petals of a fragrant water-lily
© Pam Hickman/Valan

The Flashes of 5-Island Harbor, Antigua in the Caribbean
© Gerry Ellis/Ellis Wildlife Collection

A land snail
© Bill Christensen/Root Resources

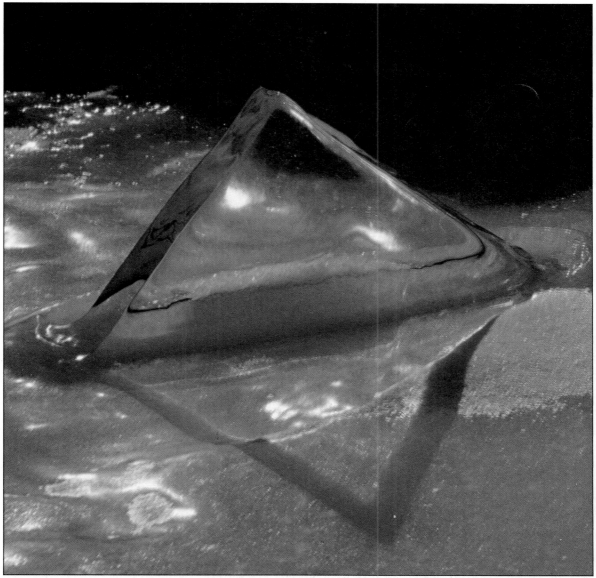

An ice prism from Bell Falls, Quebec, Canada
© Harold V. Green/Valan

A partial solar eclipse in 1972
© Conrad L. Kussner/Tom Stack & Associates

Dew drops on a blade of grass
© Rod Planck/Tom Stack & Associates

A money penny plant
Photri

The symmetrical structure of a single frost crystal
© Wilf Schurig/Valan

The open mouth of an American crocodile
© Lynn M. Stone

Ripe cherries
© Gail Nachel/Root Resources

The rock surface and Clyde Island at Eaglehawk Neck, Australia
© Tony Joyce/Valan

The honeycomb inside a beehive
© Jeff Foott/Valan

19

Delicate Arch is a highlight of Arches National Park in Utah
© David L. Brown/Journalism Services

The green skin of a Packham's Triumph pear
© Tony Joyce/Valan

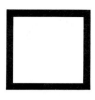

Rock formations in Monument Valley, Arizona
© Jerry Hennen

The moon over the New York City skyline
© Joe Smoljan/SuperStock International, Inc.

The leaves of violet wood sorrel
© Kerry T. Givens/Tom Stack & Associates.

Giants causeway in Northern Ireland
© Manley Photo/SuperStock International, Inc.

The face of a black rhino
© Lynn M. Stone

Sulfur crystals magnified
Photri

The spiraling tendrils of a climbing plant
© Pam Hickman/Valan

A dandelion gone to seed
© O. J. Troisfontaines/SuperStock International, Inc.

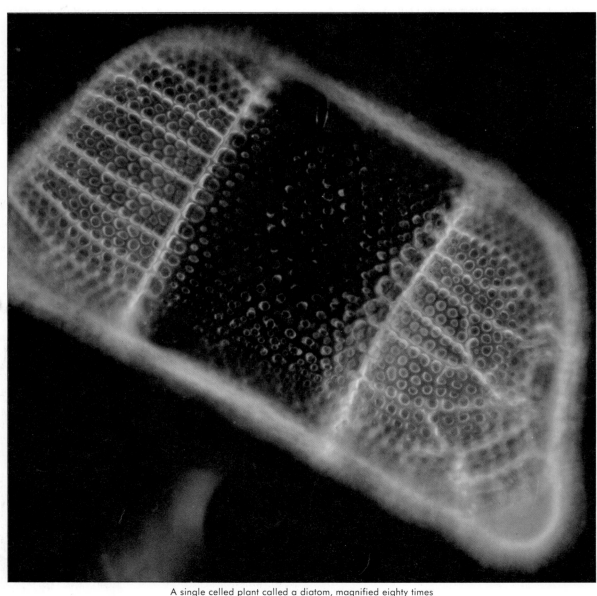

A single celled plant called a diatom, magnified eighty times
© H.V. Green/Valan

30

A red squirrel in a tree
© Jerry Hennen

triangle    oval    star    heart    petal

spiral    crescent    teardrop    snowflake    circle

square    honeycomb    arch    pear    rectangle

cone    question mark

This book has no words. It doesn't need any. The idea is for you, parents and children together, to supply the words while sharing a fun new way of looking at nature and learning about shapes.

*Judy Feldman*